North American Desert Life

Coloring Book

RUTH SOFFER

DOVER PUBLICATIONS
Garden City, New York

Bibliographical Note

North American Desert Life Coloring Book is a new work, first published by
Dover Publications in 1994.

International Standard Book Number
ISBN-13: 978-0-486-28234-3
ISBN-10: 0-486-28234-1

Manufactured in the United States of America
28234120
www.doverpublications.com

Publisher's Note

THE DESERT OF western North America is actually a patchwork of several deserts. All of course have dry climates, but they also differ in a number of ways. The northern ones are grouped roughly into what is called the desert of the Great Basin, a cooler desert that includes much of the states of Nevada, Utah, Oregon, Idaho and parts of Wyoming, Colorado and Arizona. The typical plant in the Great Basin is sagebrush.

The Mojave Desert occupies parts of southern Nevada and eastern California. It includes some of the hottest and driest regions in the country (Death Valley is here) but also some unusual vegetation, most notably the Joshua Tree.

The Chihuahuan Desert, with its mixed covering of Mesquite and various low-growing cacti, covers part of south New Mexico and west Texas but is primarily a Mexican desert, stretching through several Mexican states.

Also largely Mexican, but with a sizable chunk in southern Arizona and New Mexico, is the Sonoran Desert. Parts of this desert enjoy relatively heavy summer rains, promoting the growth of an unusual variety of plants, the most conspicuous of which is the Giant Saguaro cactus.

As you will see when you color the 44 drawings in this book, the dryness of these deserts has not prevented them from being home to a surprising variety of trees, shrubs, herbaceous plants, birds, lizards, snakes, turtles, frogs, insects, rodents, rabbits, cats and other plants and animals. Some kinds, like Porcupines, Cardinals and Yucca, are also found elsewhere; others, like Gila Monsters, Cactus Wrens and Teddy Bear Chollas, are found nowhere else.

A number of the drawings are shown in color on the covers, and alphabetical lists of common and of Latin names appear at the back of the book.

The **Chuckwalla** (*Sauromalus obesus*) is a species of Iguana and, as many people are surprised to learn, a vegetarian. These lizards, a varying blend of grays, browns and yellow, have a characteristically bloated appearance. Below are *Mammillaria* (Pincushion) cacti with showy red flowers.

Kit Fox (*Vulpes macrotis*). This smallest North American fox has a rusty gray coat. It is nocturnal and therefore rarely emerges from its burrow except at night, and then its large ears help it locate the rodents that are its chief prey. In the background are the distinctive Giant Saguaro cacti of the Sonoran Desert (see also the drawings on pages 14 and 19).

Bighorn Sheep (*Ovis canadensis*). These handsome wild sheep, brown to grayish brown with white rumps, inhabit the rocky slopes of high mountains. A mature male can weigh up to 275 pounds. The cactus at the lower right is *Coryphantha erecta*, a low-growing species found mostly in Mexico.

Striped Skunk *(Mephitis mephitis)*. This omnivorous, nocturnal mammal (that is, it will eat almost anything and is active mostly at night), black with a conspicuous white stripe, is all too familiar from the unpleasant odor it emits when disturbed. **Golden Star Cactus** *(Mammillaria elongata)*. This type of "nipple" cactus from Mexico has beautiful white flowers.

Badger (*Taxidea taxus*). Its long ears help this two-foot-long grayish brown mammal dig out its food, mostly rodents, as well as create its own burrow. The **Fairy-Duster** (*Calliandra eriophylla*), or Mock Mesquite (lower right), is a Legume, like Peas, Locust trees and Acacias. It is notable for its red-purple flowers.

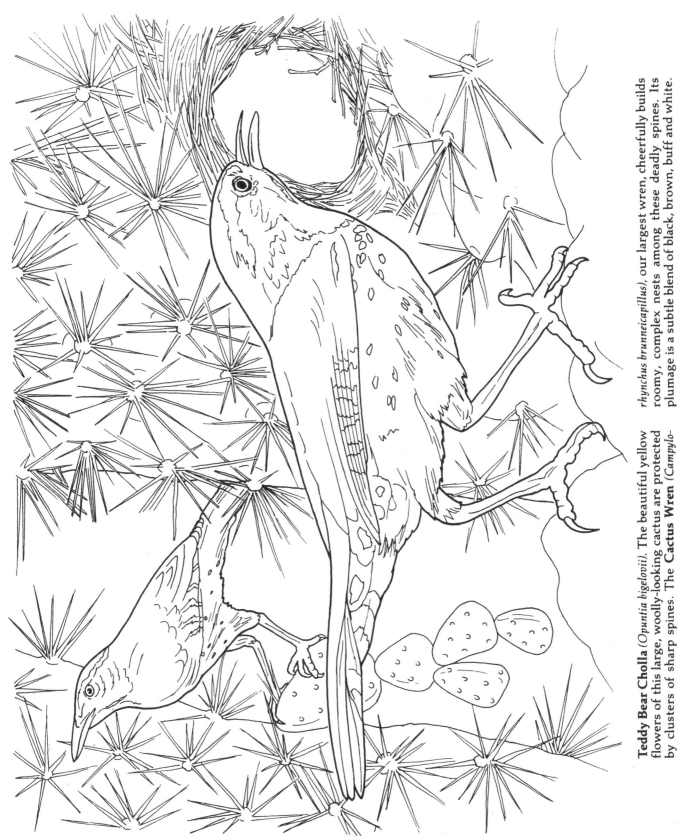

Teddy Bear Cholla (*Opuntia bigelovii*). The beautiful yellow flowers of this large, woolly-looking cactus are protected by clusters of sharp spines. The **Cactus Wren** (*Campylo-rhynchus brunneicapillus*), our largest wren, cheerfully builds roomy, complex nests among these deadly spines. Its plumage is a subtle blend of black, brown, buff and white.

The **Rock Squirrel** *(Citellus variegatus)*, with its brownish gray fur and bushy tail, resembles its cousins the tree squirrels, and, like them, it is a good climber. Its den is most frequently under a boulder rather than in a tree, which are scarce in the barren regions it inhabits.

The **Gila Monster** (*Heloderma suspectum*) is the only venomous lizard found north of Mexico (and one of only two species in the world). That fact and its colorful black, yellow, orange and pink skin have made it much better known than most lizards. The cactus at the bottom of the drawing is a type of **Prickly Pear** (*Opuntia* spp.), well known from its flattened shape. Some *Opuntia* cacti have this familiar shape, while others, with different common names, look nothing at all like this (see for example the *Opuntia* on the next page).

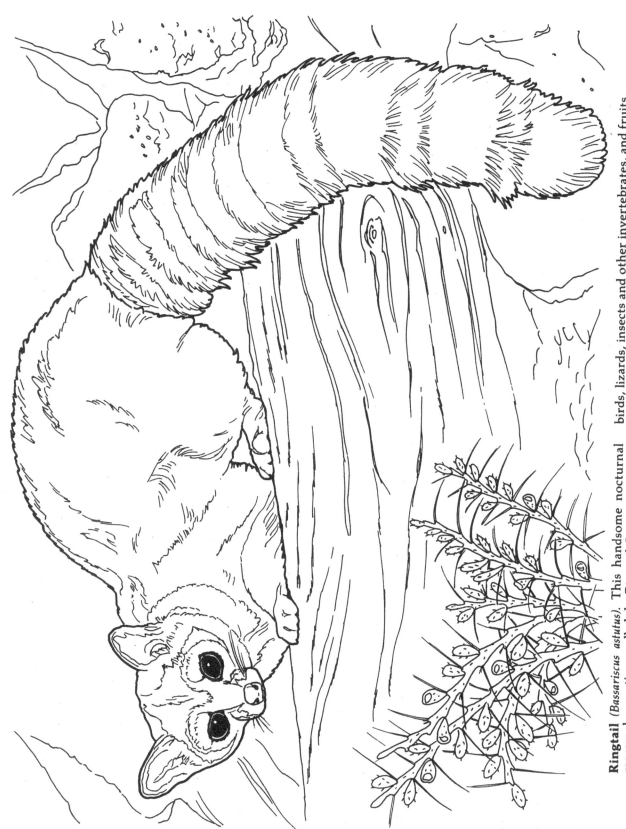

Ringtail (*Bassariscus astutus*). This handsome nocturnal mammal, sometimes called the Ringtail Cat, is not really a cat but is distantly related to the Raccoon. Its foot-long body is a pale yellowish gray; its tail is about as long, with whitish and blackish brown rings. It eats small mammals, birds, lizards, insects and other invertebrates, and fruits. **Desert Christmas Cactus** (*Opuntia leptocaulis*), found in Mexico and southern Arizona, has beautiful green-yellow flowers and bright red fruits that persist through the winter.

Porcupine (*Erethizon dorsatum*). This is the same black rodent with yellowish hairs and sharp quills known from the forests of the East. In the desert it lives in brushy areas and eats vegetable matter such as twigs and buds.

The **Giant Saguaro** cactus *(Carnegiea gigantea)* that so dominates its limited range (mostly southern Arizona and adjoining parts of Mexico) is home to **Harris' Hawk** *(Parabuteo unicinctus)*, among other creatures. Unlike those birds that live in holes in the cactus, these handsome chestnut-brown-and-white raptors build huge nests on the branches, as seen in this drawing.

The spotted brown **Bobcat** (*Lynx rufus*) is a widely distributed wildcat that feeds mostly on birds and small mammals. Though not really rare, the Bobcat is nocturnal and thus not often seen. **Turpentine Weed** (*Gutierrezia* *sarothrae*), or Turpentine Broom, is an abundant plant on arid lands at moderately high elevations. The inconspicuous yellow flowers are covered by white-to-brown bracts.

The **Turkey Vulture** *(Cathartes aura),* now found in all of the lower 48 states and even parts of Canada, is common in the Western deserts, including those of Mexico. It feeds mostly on carrion, that is, the flesh of dead animals. Here a number of vultures are shown in the Sonoran Desert in typical surroundings. Adults have a conspicuous red head.

Geckos are well known as the lizards whose tails break off when grasped. This maneuver enables them to confuse predators while they beat a hasty retreat. The mottled yellow-and-brown **Banded Gecko** (*Coleonyx variegatus*), seen here in two variants, is found in the deserts of the southwestern U.S. and adjoining parts of Mexico. It feeds on insects and spiders. *Echinocereus sciurus*, a type of **Hedgehog Cactus,** bears three-inch-long magenta flowers in the spring.

Giant Desert Hairy Scorpion (*Hadrurus arizonensis*). Scorpions (related to spiders and therefore not really insects) are much feared but many are not as deadly as people think—unless you happen to be one of the insects it eats!

The central part of the body of this species is black, the extremities yellow. **Hedgehog Cactus** (*Echinocereus pulchellus*). This small, barrel-shaped cactus (bottom) has beautiful rosy-white flowers.

Perhaps the best-known plant of the Sonoran desert, the **Giant Saguaro** cactus can live hundreds of years and grow to sixty feet. It takes several years for the characteristic branches to develop. Because ordinary trees are rare in much of the territory where the Saguaro is common, the

Gila Woodpecker *(Melanerpes uropygialis)* often makes its home in the towering cactus. The male has a red patch on his head. Both sexes have a buffy body with streaked black-and-white back.

Leafnose Bat (*Macrotus californicus*). Named for the flap of skin attached to its nose, this small grayish brown flying mammal feeds on insects and plant matter. It lives in such dark locations as abandoned mine tunnels.

The **Desert Shrew,** or Gray Shrew (*Notiosorex crawfordi*), is one of the few shrews that can tolerate an arid habitat. Like all shrews, it feeds on insects. It is paler and more ashen-colored than other shrews.

Mountain Lion (*Felis concolor*). Three to four feet long, not including tail, this tawny cat (also called Cougar and Puma) is indirectly familiar to almost everyone. Yet few have seen this secretive hunter in the wild. In the West it inhabits remote mountainous regions and feeds mostly on deer and smaller mammals. Mountain Lions very rarely attack people. The occasional unfortunate incident is usually well publicized and has caused these handsome creatures to be much maligned. The cactus is *Mammillaria longimamma*, one of about 150 species of **Pincushion Cactus,** found primarily in Mexico.

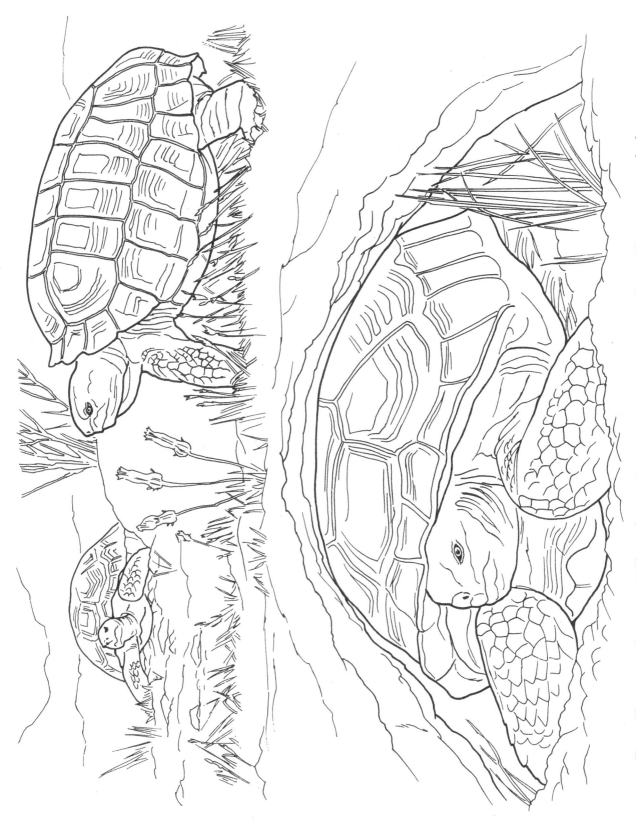

Desert Tortoise (*Gopherus agassizii*). This endangered species, ranging in size up to a foot long, its color dusky tinged with yellow, inhabits elaborate complexes of burrows in arid regions of the Southwest (the tortoise at the bottom in this drawing is seen emerging from one of these burrows). It feeds on the sparse grasses found in its territory.

The long-legged **Burrowing Owl** (*Athene cunicularia*), though chiefly nocturnal, is often seen in the daytime. It inhabits old prairie-dog burrows. Like many owls, it is brown spotted with white. Another of many types of *Mammillaria* cactus may be seen at bottom.

Whitetail Prairie Dog (*Cynomys gunnisoni*). This yellowish brown burrow-digging rodent, along with the related Blacktail Prairie Dog, was once superabundant in the semiarid parts of high-altitude Western North America. Now Prairie Dogs are harder to find, having been poisoned by humans as a result of their competition with grazing animals for food. **Indian Rice Grass** (*Oryzopsis hymenoides*). This nutritious grass (in the foreground) is a major food item of the grazing animals of the Western plains, where it occurs in abundance.

Desert Iguana (*Dipsosaurus dorsalis*). Primarily vegetarians, these reddish-brown-and-gray lizards can tolerate very high temperatures. The cactus is *Opuntia erinacea*, another type of **Prickly Pear** cactus. Its dense covering of spines gives it a hairy appearance.

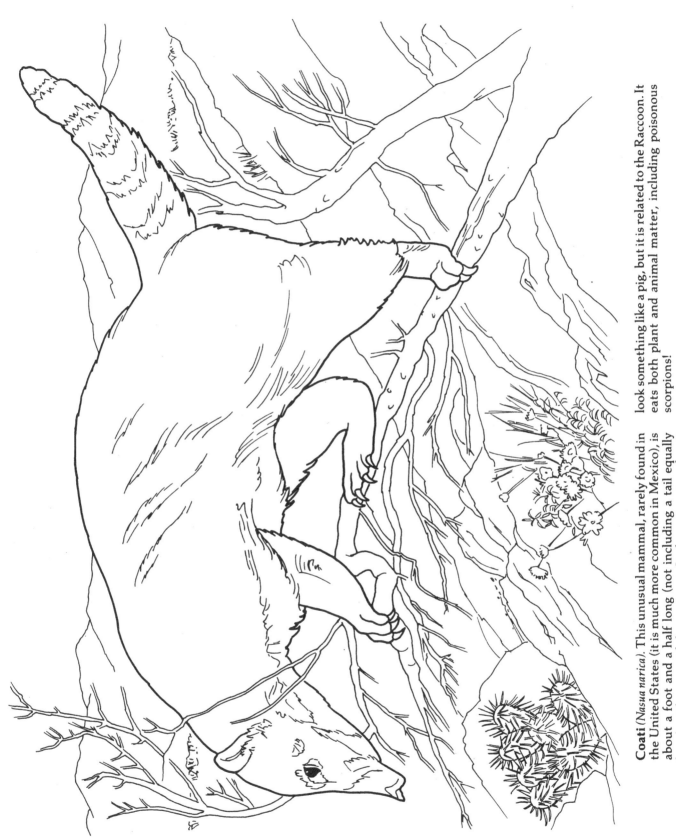

Coati (*Nasua narica*). This unusual mammal, rarely found in the United States (it is much more common in Mexico), is about a foot and a half long (not including a tail equally long) with a grayish brown coat. Its long snout makes it look something like a pig, but it is related to the Raccoon. It eats both plant and animal matter, including poisonous scorpions!

Desert Tarantula *(Aphonopelma chalcodes)*. This large, gray-brown hairy spider eats small creatures of the desert. Despite popular notions, its poison is not particularly harmful to humans. **Sand Verbena** *(Abronia fragrans)*, or Heart's Delight, is a small plant found in dry grasslands. It has beautiful lavender flowers.

Prickly Pear cactus (*Opuntia* spp.). Prickly Pears are the most widespread cacti in the Western Hemisphere (which means the world, since cacti are not naturally found elsewhere), one species even native to sandy areas as far east as Cape Cod. Prickly Pears are valuable in many ways. Their flowers are large and showy, they bear edible fruits and the pads themselves may be eaten, as many desert animals know very well.

California Quail *(Callipepla californica).* This gregarious gray-brown-white-and-black bird eats mostly seeds, with some insects. It is very common throughout much of the West. Like the California Quail, the **Four-wing Saltbush** *(Atriplex canescens)* is widespread in the West. This shrub thrives in dry, salty soils.

The **Coyote** (*Canis latrans*) is just a wild dog, yet it has about it an aura suggestive of a creature of mythology; its habit of howling at the moon makes it sound supernatural indeed. Coyotes, with their rusty brown coats, are extremely widely distributed, now found in much of the East as well as the West. They eat mostly small rodents, but at times will feed on almost anything. As common as the Coyote is, so is the strange **Boojum Tree** (*Idria columnaris*) rare, found only in the desert of Baja California (a part of Mexico adjoining California). Its long, weirdly twisting branches are like a creation of fantasy, hence the name "boojum," from Lewis Carroll's *The Hunting of the Snark*.

Mule Deer (*Odocoileus hemionus*). Its black-tipped tail and evenly branched antlers distinguish this deer from its eastern cousin the Whitetail Deer. Another characteristic is its brownish gray coat with white patches. **Big Sagebrush** (*Artemisia tridentata*), in the background, is the most common shrub in the arid and semiarid high deserts of Western North America. The shrublike herb in the foreground is **Desert Sage** (*Salvia eremostachya*), in no way related to Big Sagebrush. It is, rather, related to the herb Sage used in cooking.

This typical Western United States setting shows the **Golden Eagle** (*Aquila chrysaetos*) in its rugged home country with a solitary **Fremont Cottonwood** (*Populus fremontii*), often the only tree found in these harsh surroundings.

The Golden Eagle, its yellowish brown head slightly contrasting with an all-brown body, feeds mostly on small mammals, birds and reptiles.

Honey Ant (*Prenolepis imparis*). The ants with distended abdomens in this drawing are specialized workers called "repletes." Other honey ants gather a honeylike substance from aphids and scale insects. This honey is fed to the repletes, who store it internally for the other ants to consume at a later time. Honey ants, glossy reddish brown or black, are found throughout much of the West.

Northern Cardinal (*Cardinalis cardinalis*). These birds, familiar and much loved in the East, are found only in a few areas of the West in the United States, including parts of Texas, New Mexico and Arizona. These seed eaters (the male is bright red, the female brown tinged with red) are widespread throughout the Mexican deserts, however. The **Prickly Pear** cactus in the foreground is showing its ripe fruit.

The **Southwestern Toad** (*Bufo microscaphus*), at the top in the drawing, is found amid gravelly areas near desert watercourses. Its color ranges from olive to pink, sometimes with dark spots. Its relative the **Red-spotted Toad** (*Bufo* *punctatus*) may be olive or grayish brown and usually has reddish warts. It is the only North American toad that lays its eggs one at a time rather than in strings.

The tropical and subtropical **Peccary** *(Pecari angulatus)* is the only New World wild pig. This three-foot-long black-and-gray mammal, found in Arizona, Texas, New Mexico and Mexico (and down into South America) feeds on Prickly Pear cactus, birds' eggs, grubs and numerous other odds and ends. The cactus in the foreground is *Neolloydia subterranea,* found in the deserts of New Mexico.

Sonora Mud Turtle (*Kinosternon sonoriense*). Unlike the more terrestrial Desert Tortoise, these smaller turtles (they grow to about six inches) gather wherever they can find water. They eat snails.

One of the rarest of cats in the United States, seen only occasionally in small parts of Texas, Arizona and New Mexico, the **Ocelot** (*Felis pardalis*) is more widely distributed in Mexico. It looks something like a small Jaguar, its spots being more elongated and stripelike.

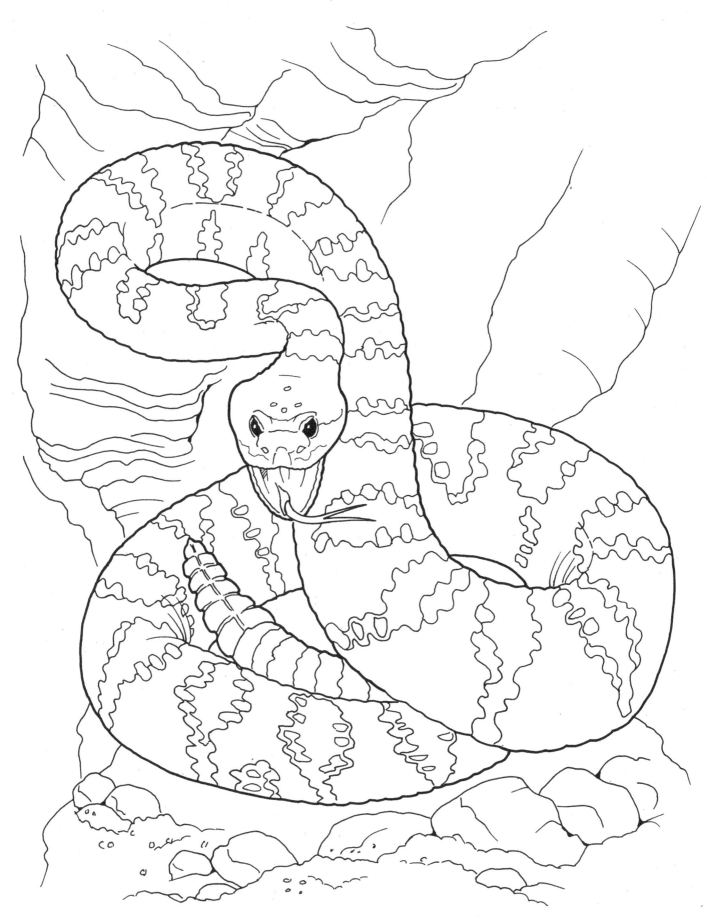

The sandy, speckled appearance of the **Speckled Rattle-snake** *(Crotalus mitchelli)* affords it good camouflage in the deserts where it is found. One of a number of rattlesnakes found in the West, it eats squirrels, lizards, mice, rats and birds.

The brilliant orange-black-and-white **Monarch** (*Danaus plexippus*), bottom, is perhaps the best-known North American butterfly. Above it are several types of **Crescentspot** butterflies (*Phyciodes* spp.), members of the huge family of Brush-footed Butterflies. The **Desert Lily** (*Hesperocallis undulata*), like the familiar lilies of gardens worldwide, has lovely, showy white flowers.

Closely related to all the smaller Yuccas that are frequently seen as ornamental plants, particularly in the South, the **Joshua Tree** *(Yucca brevifolia)* grows to over thirty feet and is a very striking part of the landscape in its limited range (part of the Mojave Desert).

Jackrabbits are really hares, not true rabbits, although both hares and rabbits belong to the same order, Lagomorphs. The **Blacktail Jackrabbit** (*Lepus californicus*) of the Western prairies and deserts is mostly brown with distinc-tive black-tipped ears as well as a black streak atop its tail. It can run at speeds of up to 35 miles per hour. Like all rabbits and hares, it is a vegetarian.

The **Desert Kingsnake** (*Lampropeltis getulus splendida*) is a member of the Colubrids, the largest family of snakes in the world. Kingsnakes are large themselves, growing to over six feet. While not poisonous or a threat to humans, they are a terror to other snakes, even rattlesnakes, which they kill by constriction (squeezing) and then eat. There are several regional variations in the appearance of this snake. The one in this drawing is dark brown with light, wavy bands. Besides other snakes it eats birds, rodents and reptiles.

The **Desert Kangaroo Rat** (*Dipodomys deserti*) is named after the desert in which it dwells (like all of the 16 or so species of Kangaroo Rats and Mice). It is yellowish and white, has a typically long tail and lives in burrows. The long, hooked spines of the tiny **Fishhook Cactus** (*Ancistrocactus scheeri*), at right, are typical of this type of cactus, found in Texas and Mexico.

The **Raccoon** (*Procyon lotor*), with its masked appearance and distinctive ringed tail, is found almost everywhere, sometimes even in the desert, especially near sources of water, in which it typically dips its food. The **Mexican Palo Verde** (*Parkinsonia aculeata*) is a distinctive member of the Legume, or Pea, family (Locusts and Acacias are other trees that belong to this family). As on other Palo Verdes, the bark is green and is capable of photosynthesis, or the use of light in a chemical reaction to provide a nutritional substance. In most plants, only the leaves can do this. The flowers of this Palo Verde are yellow, with one petal eventually turning red.

The green-and-yellow **Bullfrog** (*Rana catesbeiana*) is the largest frog in North America. It needs the presence of water; if that requirement is met it may be found even on the borders of the desert, as in this drawing. The **Star** **Cactus** (*Astrophytum ornatum*), originally found in Mexico, is cultivated elsewhere for its beautiful red-and-yellow flowers.

Alphabetical List of Common Names

Alphabetical List of Latin Names